MEMORY LANE
CARDIFF

Brian Lee

MEMORY LANE CARDIFF

Brian Lee

breedon books
PUBLISHING

First published in Great Britain in 2002 by
The Breedon Books Publishing Company Limited
Breedon House, 3 The Parker Centre,
Derby, DE21 4SZ.

ISBN 1 85983 314 4

Printed and bound by Butler & Tanner, Frome, Somerset, England.
Cover printing by Lawrence-Allen Colour Printers, Weston-super-Mare, Somerset.

Contents

Introduction

I WOULD like to thank all the people who helped me in the compilation of this book. My special thanks go to the *South Wales Echo's* cartoonist Gren Jones MBE. for writing the foreword and for producing the end-paper cartoons.

For providing me with photographs I would like to thank the following: Fred and Maureen MacCormac, Alun Williams, Les Gibbon, Alan Mitchem, P. Weston, Mary Clarke, Eric Williams, D. Riley, Owen Martin, David Thomas, George Frantzeskou, Phil Street, Bill and Betty Smith, Mike James, Emily Donovan, David Harding, R. Bord, Philip and Mary Donovan, Mr and Mrs Arthur Weston Evans, Norman Hopkins, Alan Hambly, Pam Byard, Neil Jones, Jeff Heath, Pat Collins, Peter Langham, Valerie and Malcolm Beames, Harry Ferris, Bill Barrett, Paul Crippin, Mike Thane, David Davies, FRICS of Stephenson & Alexander, Howard Anham, Gerry Latham, Glynn Pockett MBE, Dennis Pope, of Pope's Photo Services, Lex MacCormac, Christine Ashley, John Billot (former sports editor *The Western Mail*) and Russell Harvey.

I also need to thank the editors of *The Western Mail*, *South Wales Echo*, *The Post* and *The Cardiff Advertiser* for their support and all those people who provided me with photographs which, for one reason or another, were not used on this occasion.

It has not always been possible to trace the copyright of some of the photographs and I apologise for any inadvertent infringement. I also ask forgiveness of anyone I may have omitted from these acknowledgements.

A word of thanks to the staff of the Cardiff Central Library Local Studies Department for their help over the years and finally to Anton Rippon, managing director of Breedon Books, for publishing this book which, I hope, will provide Cardiffians with another lasting memorial of the city's fascinating past.

Foreword

When Brian Lee asked me to write the foreword to this book I felt I had really arrived as a Cardiffian. A valley boy (and proud of it) from Hengoed in the Rhymney Valley, I first became aware of the historic city of Cardiff at an early age from my end-of-the-valleys railway line which led to what is now the capital city of Wales.

I suppose my earliest memory of Cardiff was when, as a very young boy, I was taken by my mother to the Cory Hall in Station Terrace to attend recordings of that never to be bettered BBC Radio Wales light entertainment show *Welsh Rarebit*. I loved every minute of it. All the comedians, soloists, choirs and best of all those unforgettable and wonderful 'Tommy Trouble' sketches written by E. Eynon Evans.

A few years later, another facet of Cardiff unfolded when my Dad took me and my pal to see Cardiff City play at Ninian Park. The first game I attended was on an Easter Monday when the Bluebirds played Bristol City. And, if my memory serves me right, the crowd of 46,000 was a record one which still stands for a home game. The day was full of exciting drama and one I will never forget. One eager fan striving for a better view found it from the roof of the old Grangetown Stand. Unfortunately, he fell through the roof and the hole was there for all to see for many seasons to come.

The Bluebirds team of that era is forever with me: Canning, Lever, Sherwood, Hollyman, Stansfield, Baker, Gibson, Rees, Richards, Blair and Wardle.

Another magical place for me was the National Museum of Wales which I used to visit with my pal Brian before we went to the match. It fascinated me then and it still does today.

During the 1950s, when Cardiff City were playing away, I became aware of yet another of my great loves – Cardiff Rugby Football. Oh the sheer bliss of watching the likes of Bleddyn (Williams) and Doctor Jack (Matthews). Oval or round ball, both my teams were Cardiff then and will always be so. When the big band era arrived I went to the Sunday evening concerts at the Capitol Cinema. I saw the incredible Stan Kenton and his Orchestra, Eric Delaney, Joe Loss, Harry Gold, Eric Winstone, The Squadronaires and many other big bands.

However, my favourite, even to this day, was the fabulous Ted Heath Orchestra with singers Dicky Valentine, Denis Lotis and Lita Rosa. Around the same time came the Cinemascope blockbuster films such as *The Robe*, *Quo Vadis* and *The Great Caruso*. The queues for those epics, at least four deep, would snake halfway down Queen Street to the Capitol Cinema.

Eating out was then usually confined to a café or a coffee and doughnut in the Kardomah. But soon afterwards the first grill-type restaurants arrived and after watching a film I would shoot off to my favourite place, The Homestead, a basement grill near the corner of Churchill Way and Queen Street.

What gastronomic delights there were for one such as I who had never before encountered a mixed grill – let alone a pineapple ring on a gammon steak! And all with chips too!

It was an incredibly popular place, the queue started at street level and went down at least two flights of steep stairs before entering the restaurant and there always seemed to be a queue there. A devout curry afficionado, I had my very first down the docks (it's still the docks to me) in a dingy place called Sadies after celebrating someone's birthday in The Albert. Now years later, having spent more than half my life working in Cardiff, I have great affection for the place and gratitude for all it has given me.

It is a city big enough to be a capital and small enough for its inhabitants to still feel a real part of it. Thank you Cardiff and thank you Brian Lee for providing Cardiffians, both young and old, with another delightful walk down Cardiff's Memory Lane.

Gren Jones MBE

The Civic Centre

Cardiff's most famous landmark, the City Hall clock tower, was designed in the style of the English Renaissance by Messrs Lanchester, Stewart and Rickards.

Norman Hopkins took this picture from the clock tower in around 1980.

The City Hall, opened in 1906 by Lord Bute, is the centrepiece of the magnificent Civic Centre.

The old Town Hall was opened in St Mary Street in 1854 and was extended in 1876 to contain the post office, police court and fire brigade offices.

Another view of the City Hall and clock tower. Many Cardiffians will remember the iron chains and stone pillars around the circle in front of the City Hall.

Two views of the impressive University College in Museum Avenue, opened in 1909. The rest of the building was constructed between 1912 and 1962.

The foundation stone of the National Museum of Wales was laid in 1912 but owing to World War One, the main block and western galleries were not opened until 1927.

The Glamorgan County Hall in King Edward VII Avenue was opened in 1912 and extended in 1932.

With its portico of Doric columns the Technical College, now UWIST, was built in 1916.

Erected as a gift to the Welsh people, by the First Lord Davies, of Llandinam, the Temple of Peace was opened in 1938.

Originally opened as the Welsh Board of Health on St David's Day, 1933, the building is now the Welsh Office.

These two ladies are enjoying a stroll in the beautifully kept Queen Alexandra Gardens.

The Welsh National War Memorial which was unveiled by Edward, Prince of Wales, on 12 June 1928.

The Law Courts which were completed in 1934. The statue right of picture is that of Judge Gwilym Williams of Miskin (1839-1906).

The statue of the 3rd Marquis of Bute in Friary Gardens was unveiled in 1930.

Prime Minister Harold Macmillan unveiled the statue of David Lloyd George in 1960.

Albert Toft designed the South African War Memorial erected in memory of around 200 soldiers who were killed serving in the Welch Regiment.

Cardiff Castle

Cardiff Castle in the 1920s.

The residential area inside the castle walls.

The Norman Keep.

Cardiff Castle viewed from Kingsway.

North-west view of Cardiff Castle. The bridge built in 1879 was dismantled in 1927. It was moved to a different part of the castle grounds and demolished in 1963.

Westgate, Town Wall
rebuilt in 1921.

Above and below: The magnificent towers of Cardiff Castle as viewed from Bute Park.

The Octagon Tower.

The Lover and the Lady murals in the Summer Smoking Room.

The Summer Smoking Room.

The ornate clock
tower built
between 1867-72.

The murals depicting the life of Robert the Consul are a great feature of the Banqueting Room.

The 18th-century Drawing Room.

The Banqueting Hall.

Bute Park, Cardiff Castle grounds, were laid out by the famous landscape architect Capability Brown.

The low brick walls mark the original site of the remains of Blackfriars, a Dominican priory founded in 1242 on the left bank of the River Taff. The site was excavated in 1887 by the Marquis of Bute.

One of the 52 locks of the Glamorgan Canal. The thatched cottage which was bombed during World War Two is in centre of picture.

The Castle Lodge, North Road, which was destroyed by German bombers in March 1941, shown here *c.*1910.

The inside of Cardiff Castle walls were used as air-raid shelters during World War Two.

Remains of Roman wall at the north gate of Cardiff Castle during excavation around 1900.

City Scenes

'This is one of the big streets of Cardiff' wrote Myfanwy Jones when she sent this postcard of St Mary Street to Mrs W. Hodgson in the USA in 1923.

In this picture looking north of St Mary Street can be seen the beautiful tower of the parish church of St John Baptist, built in 1473.

Trams had been running for 25 years or more when this picture was taken in St Mary Street around 1927.

This picture was taken from almost the same spot as the above one, *c.*1963.

Bed and breakfast at the Terminus Hotel (now Sam's Bar) would have cost you 3s 6d (17½p) when this picture was taken.

'Came to Cardiff this morning arriving about ten o clock. Have been over to the docks extremely interesting. I had no idea they were so big. It's quite the way they load coal' wrote the sender of this postcard in 1905. To the right is the old town hall demolished in 1914.

The Queen's Hotel can be seen to the left of both pictures taken in the late 1950s. The hotel closed in 1974 and is now known as Elgin House.

Duke Street before it was widened in 1924.

Local legend suggests that Duke Street was named after Robert, Duke of Normandy, imprisoned in Cardiff Castle. But the name suggests an association with ducks or poulterer's shops.

Castle Street. To the left of picture can be seen Castle Arcade which runs from Castle Street to High Street. It was opened on 28 October 1849 and in 1988 it underwent a £500,000 refurbishment.

The town end of Park Place. The New Theatre is left of picture.

This view shows Queen Street and the junction of The Friary.
Mackross Stores can clearly be seen to the right of the
Principality Building Society dome, *c.*1970.

The Glamorgan County Cricket Club ground in Westgate Street, *c.*1970.

The popular Rose and Crown public house, bottom left, had occupied the same site from 1787 until it was demolished in 1974.

To the left of E.S. Chappell the Tailors stood the Electric Theatre at 37 Queen Street. The building was demolished in 1921 along with the adjoining premises to make way for Dominions House and Arcade.

Left of picture is Marments Store, Queen Street, which opened in 1879 and closed in 1986.

These two pictures of Queen Street were taken from the same place, but some years apart. Evan Roberts stood on the right of the corner of Kingsway and Queen Street from 1922 until the building was demolished in 1985. The shop with the blinds was Godfrey Musical Instruments when the top picture was taken and Masters the gents outfitters when the bottom one was taken.

Some older Cardiffians will recall the ladies and gentlemen's lavatories on Kingsway. It was near this spot that the North Gate of the old town wall once stood, *c.*1955.

Wood Street Congregational Church was demolished in 1972. It had opened as a music hall when the area was known as Temperance Town in 1864. It had seating for more than 2,200 people. The site is now occupied by Southgate House.

Hodge Building, St Mary Street. The old town hall, built on a site of land between Westgate Street and St Mary Street, was opened in 1854 and stood on this site until 1913.

A beefburger, with tomato ketchup, at Asteys self service restaurant in Park Lane in the 1970s would have cost you just 12p.

Haywood House, Dumfries Place, was being built when this picture was taken from the roof of what is now Windsor House, *c.*1978.

All the houses in Dumfries Place had been knocked down to make way for a multi-storey car park when this picture was taken in the late 1970s. St Peter's Roman Catholic Church in Roath can be seen in the centre of the picture.

Queen Street Bridge. Taken from the roof of Windsor House in the late 1970s.

The tall building on the left is Brunel House and the other building is the AA Insurance Building which was converted into luxury flats.

Whitchurch

The village, Whitchurch, in around 1903.

Bwlch-Y-Mwyalch thatched cottages, Philog Road. *c.*1903.

Old Maltsters cottages and John Lewis's the drapers shop, 1903.

When this picture of The Parade was taken before World War One, the roads and pavements had yet to be finished.

Heol Don at the turn of the century when horse and carts were still in vogue.

Velindre Road which took its name from a nearby mansion belonging to the Booker family, *c*.1920.

Whitchurch Library, designed by Messrs R. & S. Williams, was erected by Mr W.T. Morgan at a cost of £2,000 in 1904.

Two views of Park Road taken around 50 years apart from each other.

Whitchurch Railway Station. A passenger service was started around 1910.

Tynyparc Road. It has been said that the man standing against the wall is Ernest Bush, the well-known postcard photographer, *c.*1912.

Merthyr Road in around 1910.

Milwards Terrace now Merthyr Road, *c.*1908.

Milwards Terrace showing Whitchurch Brook. Trout were plentiful in the brook 100 years ago.

Whitchurch Post and Telegraph office, Merthyr Road, *c*.1920.

Merthyr Road in the 1950s.

Boots the chemist, extreme right of picture, is still in business but the cottages have been long gone.

St Mary's Church opened in 1885 and superseded a much older church which was demolished in 1904.

The lych gate, St Mary's Church, *c.*1910.

Whitchurch Common was in ancient times known as Gwaun Treoda. During World War Two the USA army was stationed on the common, *c*.1930.

Another postcard view of Whitchurch Brook.

The Glamorgan Canal near Whitchurch was filled in during the 1950s.

Whitchurch Hospital was opened in 1908 and during World War One was used as a military hospital.

Penlline Road. The wall and lych gate of St Mary's Church is left of picture, *c*.1920.

Church Road around 1910.

Two postcard views of Old Church Road taken around 1910.

A horse and cart makes its way through Merthyr Road in 1904.

The traffic lights at Merthyr Road, *c.*1960.

The old Whitchurch parish church demolished in 1904.

This picture of the site of the old Whitchurch parish church was taken by local historian Freddie MacCormac, a resident of Whitchurch.

Enjoying a pint in The Maltsters are Harry Richards, Dennis Thomas, Mac Jones, Les Gibbon and Colin Thomas, *c.*1955.

The Maltsters pub in around 1993.

The Birchgrove in Caerphilly Road dates back to the early 1770s. It was rebuilt in 1923 and was refurbished in 2001.

Ye Olde Oake, Whitchurch. The billboards in front of the restaurant tell us that this picture was taken during World War One.

Whitchurch's Billy Brian was not only Wales's greatest trick cyclist he was also an accomplished pianist. In 1904 he cycled from Newport to Cardiff non-stop, backwards!

Mellingriffith programme.

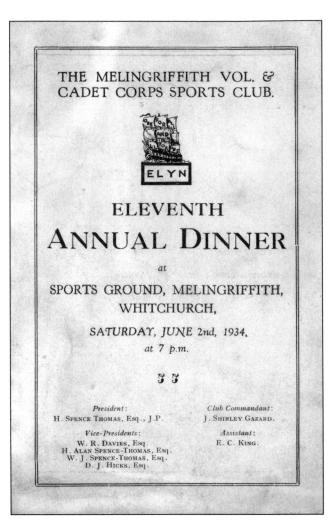

THE MELINGRIFFITH VOL. &
CADET CORPS SPORTS CLUB.

ELEVENTH
ANNUAL DINNER

at

SPORTS GROUND, MELINGRIFFITH,
WHITCHURCH,

SATURDAY, JUNE 2nd, 1934,
at 7 p.m.

President :
H. Spence Thomas, Esq., J.P.

Vice-Presidents :
W. R. Davies, Esq.
H. Alan Spence-Thomas, Esq.
W. J. Spence-Thomas, Esq.
D. J. Hicks, Esq.

Club Commandant :
J. Shirley Gazard.

Assistant :
E. C. King.

This was Woodland Terrace in 1908. It is
now known as Whitchurch Road.

Rhiwbina

Rhiwbina village in the 1950s showing the Wenallt in the background. 'The countryside was very near, at the rear of Heol-y-Deri and up Rhiwbina Hill and the Wenallt.' G. Reyland.

This picture of Rhiwbina village was taken some years later and shops can now be seen behind the Esso petrol station. 'The village had most of the shops one would need, all privately owned and with a friendly personal touch.' G. Reyland.

Work is commenced on the Rhiwbina Garden Village project. The first houses were completed in 1913. 'When I first came to Rhiwbina in 1924 I had to catch Worrells bus on the corner of City Road, come through Llanishen and down Ty Glas Road – no Inland Revenue or ROF buildings – only fields and market gardens.' Edith David.

Committee members of the Cardiff Workers Co-operative Garden Village Society Ltd. 'One great advantage of living here then was the squad of workmen employed by the Rhiwbina Village Company, who were a shield against disasters like blocked drains, frozen pipes or leaky roofs.'   Wynford Davies.

These Rhiwbina Garden Village houses were nearing completion when this photograph was taken. 'When our house was nearly ready, we moved in, as there was no electricity for a time, we did our homework by the light of rows of candles stuck on wooden boards.' Margery Fielding.

The Rhiwbina Garden Village workers who built these houses pose for a group photograph. 'Rhiwbina was very attractive in the 1940s Lon-y-Dail was a picture in Spring. Most of the houses had flowering cherries in their front gardens, and when these were in blossom, together with the vivid yellowy greens of the opening leaves on the young limes and plants, the Avenue was really a sight to behold.' G. Reyland.

Some of the first Rhiwbina Garden Village houses to be completed. 'On Christmas Eve there were several postal deliveries, parcels coming by horse-drawn dray so late it was dark, how romantic was the scene, perhaps in the snow, the postman carrying a lantern! Christmas Day also had a delivery.' Margery Fielding.

Numbers 21 to 23 Lon-y-Dail. In 1931 after a great rainstorm a number of these houses were flooded. 'Lon-y-Dail was in those days the home of several well-known residents including Edward Lewis the solicitor, Professors Brett (English), Gruffyd (Welsh), Grundy (Latin) and Mr R.T. Jenkins, History Master at Cardiff High School for Boys.' Marjorie Lewis.

The allotments at Y Groes in the 1920s. 'Having been born in Y Groes I have many varied memories of happenings in the village over the years. Of dancing around the Maypole at the May Day celebrations which took place every year on the green at Y Groes, with a May Queen chosen by the Committee, presumably from the bevy of beauties living in the village.' S. Morgan.

Pen-y-Dre in the 1920s. 'We had our own policeman who lived in the village. Affectionately known as Copper Lewis, he knew most of the residents and was available at any time.' R. Barlow.

Numbers 1 to 19 Lon Isa. 'David Broome's father Fred used to call on us delivering greengroceries with a horse and cart then he took a shop in the village.' Mrs Audrey C. Williams.

Numbers 18 to 24 Pen-y-Dre. 'One Sunday morning as the hunt moved off down the road we watched from our front garden, to our amazement to see our wire-haired terrier trotting along with the hounds.' R. Barlow.

Pen-y-Dre in the 1920s. 'The bread and milk were brought to the door. The bread from Idris Evans of Whitchurch by a man we knew only as Charley.' Trevor Jenkins.

A feature of these houses in Pen-y-Dre, formerly Homfray Road, is the footbridges leading to the dwellings right of picture, c.1926. 'Sir Harry Secombe came to the Scouts Hall and gave a marvellous performance in aid of the Memorial Hall.' Mrs Audrey C. Williams.

Smarts Tea Gardens, owned by Mr & Mrs William Smart, was built in 1916. It had an avairy and a putting green and was very popular with courting couples.

Also known as Rhiwbina Tea Gardens a garage was added to the buildings in 1919. 'My mother remembers Tessie O'Shea as a little girl coming to Rhiwbina Tea Gardens (Smarts Garage) and singing and dancing there. What fun we had there on the swings and looking at the animals – monkeys, rabbits and birds I think. We used to go in through a turnstile for a penny.' Mrs Audrey C. Williams.

Beulah Road in the 1950s. 'Shopping in those days was like visiting a round of friends.' W.E. Gray.

View from the Wenallt. The docks and steel works can be seen in the background.

Two views of Cardiff from the Wenallt. From its highest point, 730 feet above sea level, an extensive view of the city and Bristol Channel is obtained.

City of the Parks

The Captain Scott memorial lighthouse clock tower was unveiled in 1918.

This was how the promenade looked before the erection of the Captain Scott memorial.

The figurehead of the *Terra Nova*, the ship that took Captain Scott on his ill-fated expedition to the South Pole, was displayed in Roath Park.

Generations of Cardiffians have enjoyed Roath Park's many facilities since it was opened by the Earl of Dumfries, the Rt Hon John Crichton Stuart on his 13th birthday on 20 June 1894.

Roath Park attracts 1.5 million visitors every year making it one of Wales's most popular attractions.

The Bandstand. Over the years, Roath Park has been the venue for concerts, open air dancing, carnivals and many other kinds of entertainment.

Roath Park has been a popular place for a walk (or a jog) with people from all over Cardiff in summer or winter, *c.*1920.

On 8 April 1895, Councillor G. Beynon Harris brought forward a motion in favour of permitting boating on Roath Park Lake on Sundays. But a Nonconformist deputation protested against the proposal and the motion was defeated.

In an 1897 Guide to Cardiff a season's fishing ticket to Roath Park was advertised at 5s (25p) and a rod licence a shilling (5p). In those days the trout were reared in the park's own hatchery.

Roath Park has always been a centre of horticultural excellence.

Two aerial views of Roath Park's famous rose gardens, *c.*1960.

Roath Park has seen many changes since this postcard picture was taken at the turn of the centenary.

It's springtime in Roath Park and the daffodils have put a smile on this young lady's pretty face.

Cefn Onn Park with its 200 acres of wooded hillside is a riot of colour and beauty.

The Wenallt is another park north of the city popular for rambles and picnics.

The Avenue, Sophia Gardens. The grounds were open to the public in 1858.

The first grandstand to be erected in a Cardiff park was the one in Grange Gardens, Grangetown, erected in 1895.

The Boy with a Butterfly statue in Thompsons Park has been vandalised on several occasions over the years. The park was presented to the people of Cardiff by Charles Thompson in 1911.

Despenser Gardens, Riverside, c.1955.

Plasturton Gardens in Edwardian times. A postcard view by Ernest T. Bush.

Just like the one that used to be in Roath Park, the old iron horse at Pen-y-Dre which gave so much pleasure to countless young children is long gone.

The open air swimming baths in Llandaff Fields, opened to the public in 1897, are just a memory now.

Youngsters enjoying themselves in Victoria Park's swimming pool in the 1950s.

The legendary Billy the Seal was found in a fish-box off a Neale & West trawler in 1912 was a resident in Victoria Park until it died in 1939.

Royal Visitors

COUNTY BOROUGH OF CARDIFF.

VISIT OF HIS ROYAL HIGHNESS

The Prince of Wales, K.G.

THURSDAY, 29th JUNE, 1905.

OFFICIAL PROGRAMME.

Presentation of the Honorary Freedom of the County Borough of Cardiff,

AND

Inspection of the Cardiff Railway Company's Docks,

AND

The Dowlais Iron and Steel Works of Messrs. Guest, Keen and Nettlefolds, Limited.

ROBERT HUGHES,
Mayor.

J. L. WHEATLEY,
Town Clerk.

Official programme for the visit of the Prince of Wales on 29 June 1905.

The Prince of Wales.

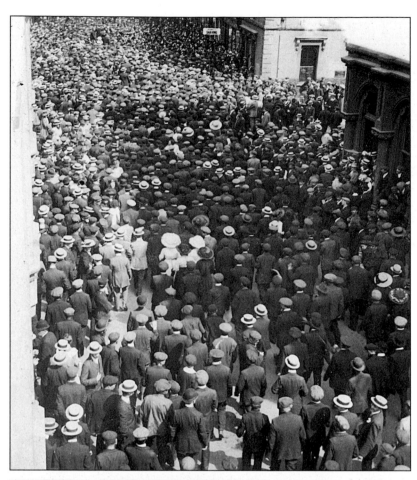

Thousands of Cardiffians descended on Cardiff docks in the hope of getting a glimpse of King George V and Queen Mary on their coronation visit to Cardiff on 25 June 1912.

King George V inspects the troops lined up at Cardiff docks.

King George VI and Queen Elizabeth in Westgate Street during their coronation visit on 14 July 1937. Thousands of well wishers await them at the famous Cardiff Arms Park.

HRH Princess Margaret visited Llandaff Cathedral on 26 February 1958.

The Queen and Prince Philip chat to the Lord Mayor, Councillor Edwards in the City Hall, 29 November 1980.

Princess Anne shakes hands with Harry Crippin, Chief Executive and Town Clerk in Cardiff Castle. Also in the picture are the Lord Mayor and Lady Mayoress, Sir Cennydd Traherne and, far right, Mrs Crippin.

HRH Princess Diana shaking hands with Mrs Crippin wife of Chief Executive Harry Crippin. The Prince of Wales looks on. It was in 1981 that Diana received the Freedom of the City.

Harry Crippin, Carolyn Watkiss the Lady Mayoress, the Prince and Princess of Wales, and the Lord Mayor Ron Watkiss CBE, 29 October 1981.

The Duke and Duchess of York at Cardiff Castle, with the Lord Mayor, Julius Hermer, c.1987.

Queen Elizabeth, the Queen Mother, officially opened St David's Hall Theatre in 1983. She is seen in both pictures with the Lord Mayor, Phil Dunleavy.

The Prince of Wales shakes hands with Mrs Harry Crippin at the Faculty of Medicine Dinner at the City Hall on 18 June 1981.

The visit of the Duchess of Gloucester to the City Hall, May 1981

Other Famous Faces

Pope John Paul II visited Cardiff on 2 June 1982. He is seen here with the Lord Mayor, Phil Dunleavy.

Cliff Richard, now Sir Cliff, attended a charity dinner at the Angel Hotel in January 1981. He is seen here with Mrs Harry Crippin.

Welsh opera singer Sir Geraint Evans (1922-1992) with the Chief Executive Harry Crippin at the City Hall, *c.*1985.

Welsh singer Tom Jones
enjoys a joke with Mrs
Harry Crippin, *c.*1983.

Two Welsh rugby
greats. Gareth
Edwards and
J.P.R. Williams
enjoying a drink
at Cardiff Castle
with Mr Harry
Crippin,
September 1978.

Prime Minister James
Callaghan, holding
South Wales Echo, with
Lord Brooks and
Harry Crippin at the
opening of the STAR
Leisure Centre, July
1981.

Prime Minister James
Callaghan, MP for Cardiff
South East, with Lord Mayor
William Carling before the
General Election results. The
Prime Minister's wife Audrey is
in the background, 3 May 1979.

Chief Executive Harry Crippin met many famous people during his years of office. He is seen here with singer Anita Harris in the City Hall, *c*.1980.

On the occasion of the opening of St David's shopping centre, a reception was given in the City Hall. Left to right are councillor Stefan Terlezki, Geraint Stanley James, controller BBC Wales, Geoff Rich, editor, *South Wales Echo*, Harry Crippin, Joe Gormley, late Lord Gormley, president National Union of Miners, March 1982.

International singing star Shirley Bassey from Cardiff is the centre of attraction at a City Hall function. Below: Left to right are Harry Crippin, Mrs Wyn Calvin, Wyn Calvin and Emmanuel who designed the Princess of Wales's wedding gown, *c.*1990.

Prime Minister Margaret Thatcher was the guest of honour at the CBI dinner on 11 December 1980.

The ever-controversial Jeffrey Archer signing the visitors book in the Lord Mayor's parlour, City Hall. Looking on is Harry Crippin and Lord Mayor Julius Hermer, 1987.

Astronomer Patrick Moore and TV star Dermot Kelly seem to be casting a spell on Lord Mayor, Albert William Buttle.

Leslie Crowther smiles for the photographer and best-selling Welsh author Leslie Thomas gives Lord Mayor Julius Hermer a few writing tips. Lord Taverners' Christmas lunch, 14 December 1987.

Transports of Delight

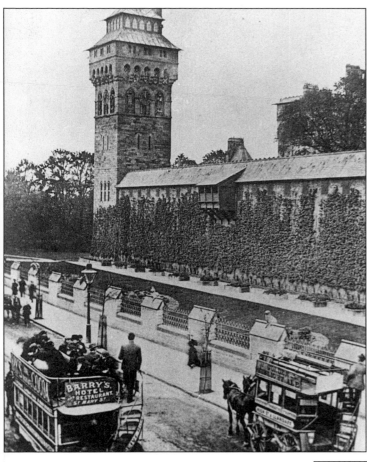

Horse-drawn buses, as seen in this picture, were the first mode of public transport in Cardiff at the turn of the century.

Horse-drawn carriages were certainly the order of the day when this picture was taken.

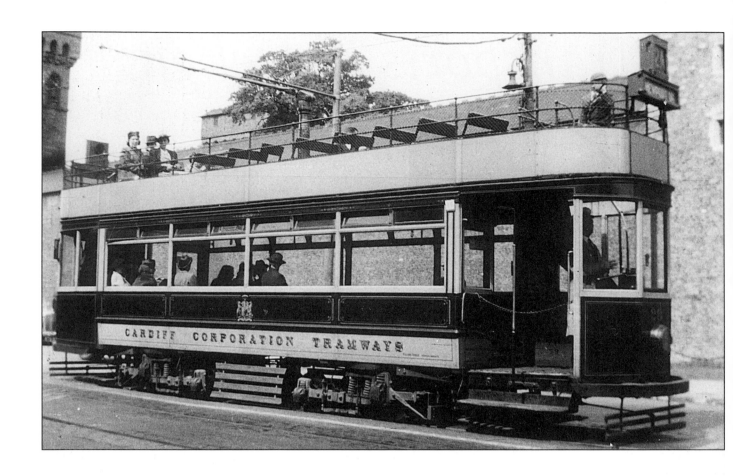

Electric tram enthusiast John C. Gillham took these two photographs of the trusty tram which transported Cardiffians to work and play between 1902-50.

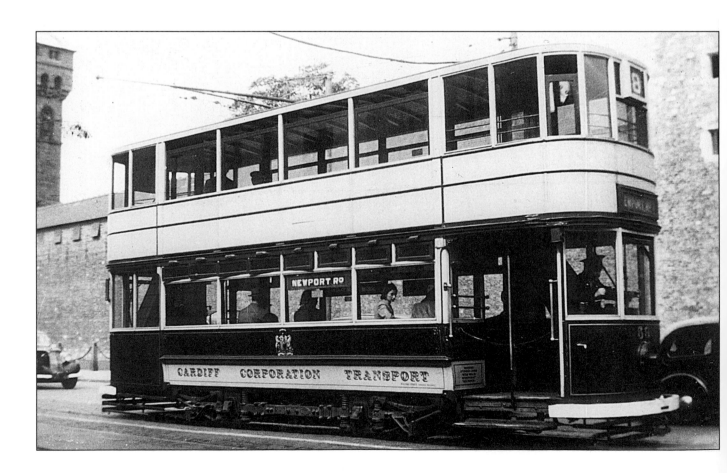

The tramcar in both these pictures is number 112 and is seen travelling down Whitchurch Road. Both photographs were taken by H.B. Priestly in the August of 1939.

Two more photographs taken by H.B. Priestly. The top one is of tramcar 119 which is seen passing the Heath Hotel in the April of 1927. The bottom picture shows a reconditioned open-topped tramcar number 30, August 1939.

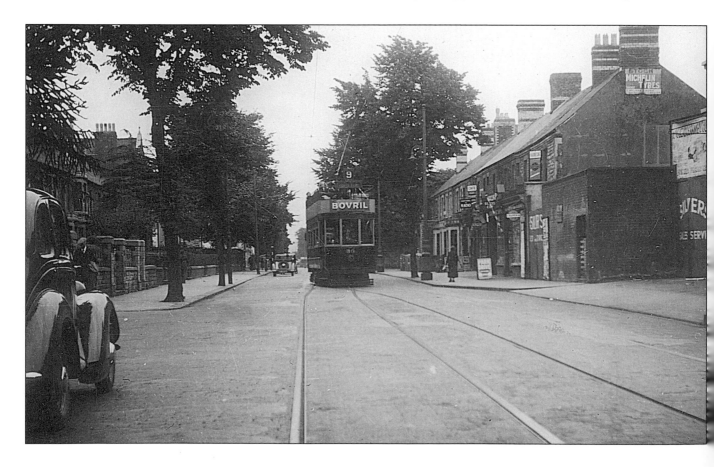

Tramcar number 81 passing the Bon Marche stores in Crwys Road, December 1937.

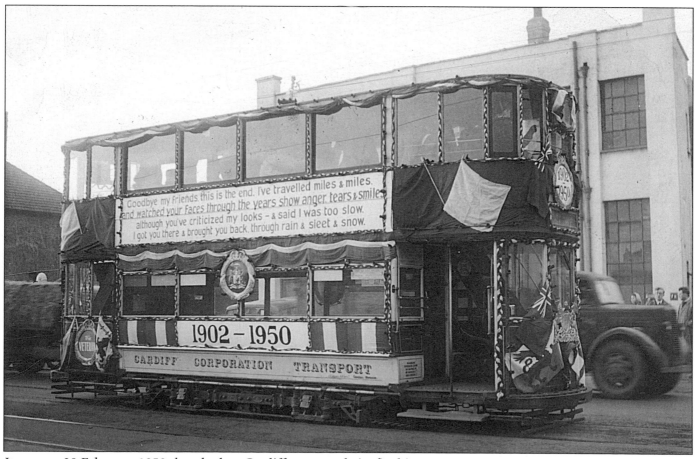

It was on 20 February 1950 that the last Cardiff tram made its final journey.

Police cars at Canton police station in 1945.

Cardiff Corporation decided to replace tramcars with trolley-buses in 1939 but owing to the outbreak of the war it wasn't until March 1942 that they were seen on the roads. The final trolley-bus to operate in the city was a specially decorated one on 11 January 1970. The one in this picture is seen passing the Royal George pub on the corner of Crwys Road and City Road.

Leckwith Bridge which was opened by Sir Leslie Hore-Belisha, Minister of Transport and inventor of the Belisha Crossing, in 1935.

When this picture was taken in the 1930s, only two cars are be seen at the junction of Sloper Road and Leckwith Road.

The Three Arches Railway Bridge at Heath, 1904. The area is now a built up one with the popular The Three Arches pub just a few yards away.

Clarence Road Bridge was opened by the Duke of Clarence in 1890. It was replaced by a new bridge in 1976.

An early photograph of Heath Halt railway station, *c.*1920.

Penarth Road toll bridge. To the left can be seen the old pumphouse now an antiques centre.

The Western Avenue Cathedral Bridge over the River Taff was opened by the Lord Mayor Charles Fletcher Sanders on 11 July 1933.

Shopping Around

Queen Street in the 1930s before the Imperial Cinema, right of picture, became the Odeon.

When this picture was taken of Queen Street in the 1940s, there was a sale at Seccombes left of picture which closed in 1977.

This was St Mary Street in the 1920s. The awnings on the shops, right of picture, were most important in those days before refrigeration when produce was displayed outside the shops.

In this picture of St Mary Street, James Howell & Co is right of picture. The entrance to the Central Market is just under H. Samuel's clock (centre), *c.*1923.

Calders on the corner of Queen Street and Churchill Way, January 1983.

Like Calders, in the above picture, these buildings were demolished to make way for the Capitol Exchange shopping complex.

The Continental Delicatessen and the Greyhound Hotel in Bridge Street shortly before they were knocked down, 1981.

The popular Dutch Café in Queen Street was taken over by Halford in the 1950s. The plaques of the Dutchmen were preserved when the building was demolished and they have been incorporated into the brickwork of the Capitol Exchange complex in Station Terrace.

W.E. & E. Walker Hay
and Seed merchants,
North Road,
Kingsway. Right of
picture is the Red
Lion Hotel, *c.*1908.

F.W. Woolworth & Co.
Clifton Street, *c.*1938.

Gooch's Hardware Stores, Beulah Road, Rhiwbina, long before decimalisation. When this picture was taken the wheelbarrow in the bottom picture would have set you back 39s 6d (less than £2 in today's currency).

A.W. Pope the confectioner is holding his youngest son Reuben in the window of his Cowbridge Road East shop while the rest of his family, and two assistants, stand outside to have their photographs taken, *c*.1906.

Mr Pope's son, Charles Pope, started his photographic business in 1924 and it is still trading today being run by his son Dennis Pope and Dennis's daughter Debbie.

Thane's Garage and by-cycle shop, 69 Caerphiliy Road, Birchgrove. The shop is now owned by Mr Phillip Thane's son Michael.

Nowell & Lewis's corner shop in Hunter Street in 1969.

Special Occasions

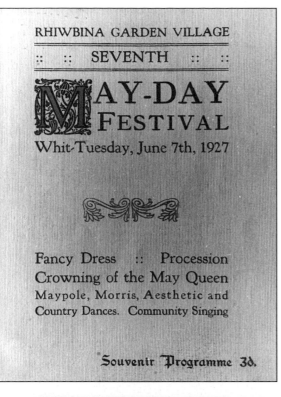

RHIWBINA GARDEN VILLAGE

:: :: SEVENTH :: ::

MAY-DAY FESTIVAL

Whit-Tuesday, June 7th, 1927

Fancy Dress :: Procession
Crowning of the May Queen
Maypole, Morris, Aesthetic and
Country Dances. Community Singing

Souvenir Programme 3d.

The seventh May Day Rhiwbina Garden Village Festival took place on 7 June 1927.

Miss Mary Williams was crowned the May Queen by her predecessor Miss Kathleen Dawes.

Town crier Alwyn Lloyd, right of picture, gave a proclamation and recited John Masefield's poem *Laughter and be Merry*.

This young lad attracted a large crowd with his country dancing.

Country dancing on the Green.

May Queen Miss Mary Williams with her attendants either side of her.

These Rhiwbina village May Day celebrations are believed to have taken place a year earlier in 1926.

A 'throwing the wellie' competition was just part of the Whitchurch silver jubilee celebrations. Fred MacCormac, hands on head, was the judge.

Gillian Collins, aged seven and a half, presenting a bouquet to Mrs Presswood the wife of Mr Presswood, Director of Education, at the opening day of Greenhills School Summer Fare, Rhiwbina. Also standing is the headmistress, Miss Chapman.

Members of Whitchurch Rugby Club's annual walk celebrations in Penlline Road, *c.*1970.

These founder members of Rhiwbina ladies croquet section would probably have been shocked by the antics of the young ladies in the above picture.

In October 1988, Lord Mayor Bill Herbert invited members of the City Hall based Historic Records Project to the Lord Mayor's parlour for the launch of *A Cardiff Notebook*. Left to right are Woke Amadi Nnah, Coordinator Brian Lee, Lee Thompson and Malcolm Lewis former head reader at the *Western Mail*, October 1988.

Lord Mayor Bella Brown, CBE, opens the Public Dispensary For Sick Animals in Cardiff, 1 July 1979.

Hollywood film star Ray Milland (Reginald Truscott) originally from Neath laid a wreath at the Welsh National War Memorial on Remembrance Sunday, 11 November 1946. A year earlier he had won an Oscar for *The Lost Weekend*.

King George VI lays a wreath at the Welsh National War Memorial in Alexandra Gardens. Standing in front of him is park keeper Bill Smith, 14 July 1937.

His Royal Highness The Duke of Edinburgh was admitted as an honorary freeman of the City and County Borough of Cardiff on 1 December 1954. Watching the Duke signing the freeman's roll is park keeper Bill Smith who was injured during World War One at Gallipoli. Mr Smith was a park keeper for 35 years.

Bill Smith at the Welsh National War Memorial with the Lord Mayor of Cardiff and other civic dignitaries one Remembrance Sunday in the 1950s.

Members of
Llanishen Baptist
Church Youth Club
on a ramble to Cefn
Onn in the 1950s.

Oxford Street celebrate the
Queen's coronation with a
street party for the children,
1953.

Llanishen Baptist church members at their annual Whitsun Treat. In the picture are Jason Porter, Val Tatchell, Jean Alward, Enid Lewis, Gaynor Smith, Cliff Colledge, Rosemary Davies, John Drewit, Neil Witts, 'Taffy' Reynolds, Ann Roberts and Howard Burge, c.1957.

Patrons of The Philog, Whitchurch, and their children before setting out on a charabanc outing, c.1950.

The National Pageant of Wales held at Sophia Gardens in 1909 attracted 175,000 spectators. The history of Wales from the 1st century to Henry VIIIs Act of Union was re-enacted by hundreds of actors.

The Marchioness of Bute (centre) as 'Dame Wales' and 'a number of ladies of high social distinction' took part in the opening ceremony.

Mr Morgan Williams as Prince Llwelyn the Great.

Mr Philip Bassett as his ancestor Bassett of Beaupre.

Mr R. Graham as King Arthur and Mr Ifano Jones as Merlin the Arch-Druid.

The Pavane danced by ladies and courtiers in this scene was a very attractive feature of the pageant.

This scene depicted the storming of Cardiff Castle by Ivor Bach in AD 1158. Some 500 Welsh football players appeared as Welsh clansmen.

This magnificent spectacle depicted the Act of Union between England and Wales AD 1536. Henry VIII was played by Mr W.T. Morgan and Queen Jane Seymour by Miss Gethin Lewis.

Between 4,000 and 5,000 people took part in the closing ceremony and at a given signal fairies joined hands to form a map of the counties of Wales.

Around and About

St John's Church in Trinity Street, the old church in the city centre has long been a popular landmark. Originally built in the 12th century, it was rebuilt in 1473.

The Ebenezer Chapel in Ebenezer Street was built in 1880 and demolished in 1974.

Penarth Road at the turn of the century. The notice on the lamppost reads 'To Weighbridge'.

City Road before the Gaiety Cinema was built in 1912. In the centre can be seen the Royal George hotel.

Left of picture is one of the two cooling towers at the Colchester Avenue Power Station, both of which were demolished in 1972.

Highcroft, Newport Road. Miss Trudy Inseal lived there until 1949. This picture was taken around 1950. Later a police station was built near the site.

Kingsway. The Rose and Crown pub, demolished in 1974 and right of picture, will be fondly remembered by many Cardiffians, *c.*1950.

The walls of Cardiff Prison, opened in 1857, can be seen centre of this picture taken under the former Rhymney Railway Bridge in Adam Street, *c.*1965.

The site of the old Maindy Pool, which claimed the lives of a number of people, after it had been filled in with 16,000 cart loads of household rubble to prepare the site for a stadium.

An athletics meeting in progress at Maindy Stadium, 1951.

Carnegie Cathays Branch Library. It was opened on 7 March 1901. One of two branch libraries presented to Cardiff by Andrew Carnegie, it cost £5,356 to build.

Penylan Court. This fine family residence was demolished some years ago. Not far from this house was a celebrated well or spring known as Hen Ffynon. After the Easter Monday fair, the well would be filled with bent pins in the belief that to drop a bent pin in the water would bring good luck.

Pier Head, Cardiff Docks. Note the tram lines. The first electric trams ran from City Road, formerly Castle Road, to the docks in 1902.

The junction of the Glamorgan Canal north end of West and East Docks, 1965.

Sporting Moments

St Saviours Harriers cross country team 1912. The club's star runner was E.J. Davies who joined Roath (Cardiff) Harriers when the club folded the following year.

Roath (Cardiff) Harriers cross country team. Seated fourth right is the legendary Ted Hopkins awarded the OBE in 1975 for his services to athletics.

Elyn Harriers, runners up in Welsh Novice Cross Country Championship 1932. Back row: I. Gaylord (senior), I. Gaylord, E. Hurford, D.J. Roberts. Front row: I. Brown, F.C. Brooks, W.E. Baker, J.P. Collard, R. Thomas. Seated second from right is Jack Collard who with Jim Thomas were the men behind Birchgrove Harriers which eventually merged with Roath Harriers in 1968 to become Cardiff AAC.

Elyn Harriers cross country team. Back row: I. Gaylord (senior), G. Tout, J.P. Collard, G. Thomas, D.J. Roberts, B. Trigg, W.E. Baker, B. Janes, E. Hurford. Front row: W. Asplin, L. Thomas, D. Hicks, I. Gaylord, P. Gazard, R.E. Baker, G. Mealing.

Cardiff University boxing team 1930. Unfortunately the boxers' names are not known.

Cardiff Nomads AFC. Combination League First Division, c.1958. In the picture are Ken and Eric Williams, Jimmy Losden, Jim Ellaway, Frank Laine, Des Lansdowne, Owen Martin, Dennis Eade.

Melingriffith Rugby Team, February 1952.

The Philog skittle team. All the players were members of the Pudge family, c.1947.

Terry Pudge from Whitchurch who was Welsh and British schoolboy champion in the 1930s.

Joe Pudge who also boxed professionally as Joe Douglas.

Les Gibbon, a nephew of Joe Pudge, who was Welsh schoolboy champion in 1945 and Welsh junior champion 1943-9.

One of Britain's best light-heavyweight champions Jack Petersen from Cardiff is seen sparring. Born 2 September 1911, he died 22 November 1999.

Local rider David Thomas aboard Miss Balscadden (22), the eventual winner, leads the field in the 1926 Welsh Grand National. Inset: David Thomas.

Harry Llewellyn, of showjumper Foxhunter fame, later Sir Harry, being led in by Wilfred Morgan after winning on China Sea at Ely Racecourse, November 1937. Mr Morgan's son Dennis is the well-known Cardiff author and local historian.

Cardiff City police swimming and water polo team, *c.*1930.

Cardiff City Police water polo team, 1950. Roy Webb, Glynn Pockett, Bert Williams, Jock Dobson, Ted Golding. Seated: Arnold Cooper, Bert Davies (superintendant), John Parkman.

Cardiff City Police AFC, *c.*1950.

Cardiff City Police AFC, 1946-7. G. Reed, C. Smith, B. Phillips, D. Harris, J. Dobson, W. Mullett. Seated: I. Jenkins, L. Holley, T. Lewis (captain), F. Bulpin. A. Summers.

Cardiff City Police AFC, 1962-3.

Cardiff City Police RFC, 1961. Back row: Frank Sallish, B. Richards, T. O'Shea, Ben Gunn, Tug Wilson, M. Brown, J. Cotterrell, B. Postans, A. Davies, L. MacCormac. Front row: C. Rayer, P. Frost, M. Brown, G. Smith, R. Hill, D. Ewington.

Cardiff City
Police Women's
Life Saving team,
c.1955.

Cardiff City Police Rifle Team, *c*.1960.

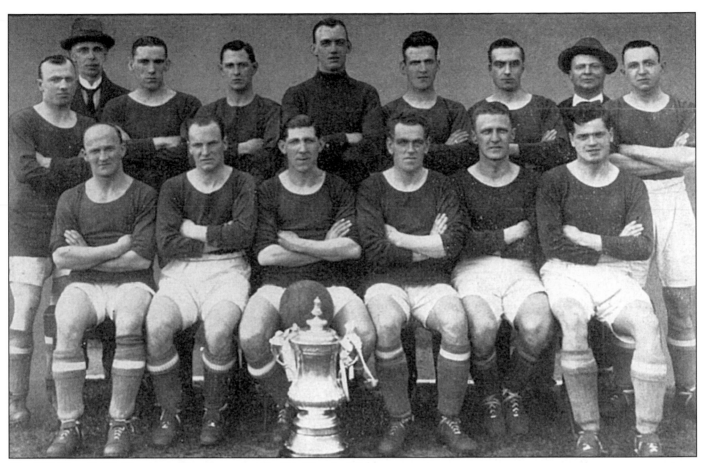

Cardiff City, 1927. The team that brought the FA Cup to Wales.

The football player reading the *Daily Mirror* is John Charles, 'The Gentle Giant'. The other Cardiff City and Wales players are, left to right: Barrie Hole, Trevor Peck, Steve Gammon, Derek Tapscott and Sandy Milner, *c.*1955.

Seating steward pass for the V1 British Empire and Commonwealth Games.

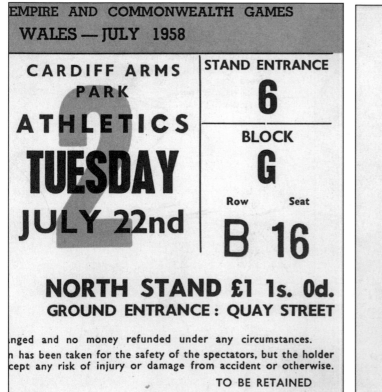

Entrance ticket for the athletics events on 22 July 1958.

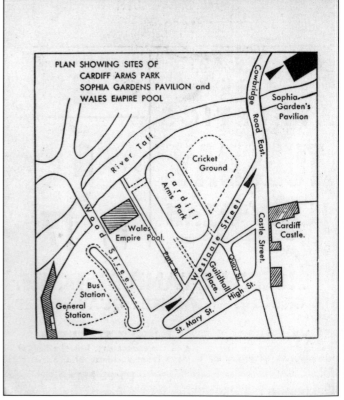

1958 British Empire and Commonwealth Games opening ceremony.

Cardiff boxer Malcolm Collins carrying the Welsh flag at the opening ceremony. To his right in tracksuit (arms folded) is Brian Lee who was one of the escort runners to Ken Harris (wearing white tracksuit), who passed the Queen's message to former Olympic Games sprinter Ken Jones, who in turn handed it to HRH the Duke of Edinburgh.

Philip Donovan took this picture of his 45-year-old nephew Brian Lee finishing the 1981 Western Mail Marathon. The course proved to be 700 yards too long and in a huge field of nearly 4,000 runners, the author finished a creditable 135th, clocking 3 hours 13 minutes 14 seconds.

Television personality Jimmy Saville (wearing number 3500) and his minders have a few more yards to run in the Western Mail Marathon, *c.*1983.

Magic hands. Gareth Edwards, who took over the captaincy when Brian Price withdrew because of injury, scoops up an untidy feed during a dazzling Welsh victory 30-9 against England at the famous Cardiff Arms Park in 1969. So Wales won the Triple Crown for the 11th time. This was the match in which Cardiff wing Maurice Richards crossed for four tries to equal the Welsh record.

They beat the All Blacks. This was the Cardiff team, captained by the great Bleddyn Williams, that triumphed 13-8 against New Zealand at the Cardiff Arms Park on 19 December 1953. Standing left to right: Gareth Griffiths, John Llewellyn, Eddie Thomas, Malcolm Collins, John Nelson, John D. Evans. Seated: Derek Williams, Stan Bowes, Rex Willis, Sid Judd, Bleddyn Williams, Cliff Morgan, Alun Thomas, Gwyn Rowlands, Geoff Beckingham.

Cardiff's squad who won the Snelling Sevens at Rodney Parade in 1984. They defeated Newport 30-12 in the final. Mark Ring was named outstanding player to win the Bill Everson Award. Standing (left to right): Tudor Jones (physio), Roger Beard, Mark Ring, Adrian Hadley, Gerald Cordle, Nathan Humphreys, Jose Souto, Stan Bowes (club chairman). Front: Kevin Hopkins, Neil O'Brien, Terry Charles (capt), Howard Stone, Owen Golding.

Bleddyn Williams hurdles South African centre Ryk van Schoor in 1951 to score Cardiff's spectacular try. It was an epic encounter, won 11-9 by the Springboks with a try five minutes from the end.

Cardiff captain Gerald Davies, dynamic wing with his devastating late swerve, swings a polished pass away during an attack against Swansea at St Helen's in April 1976. The match was drawn 11-all.

Terry Holmes, the Iron Man at scrum half, unloads to his backs against the Barbarians at the Cardiff Arms Park in 1983. Teammates Terry Charles (left) and Owen Go1ding are on hand.

Take that! Wales and Cardiff outside half Jonathan Davies fends off an intended half-tackle by England's Rob Andrew at Twickenham in 1986, when England edged a 21-18 victory.

Left: Barry John, The King, playing for the Lions in New Zealand in 1971. The Cardiff outside half was the great decision maker in a back division of unsurpassed brilliance.

Right: Another master tactician was Gareth Davies, scorer of a record 3,117 points for Cardiff.

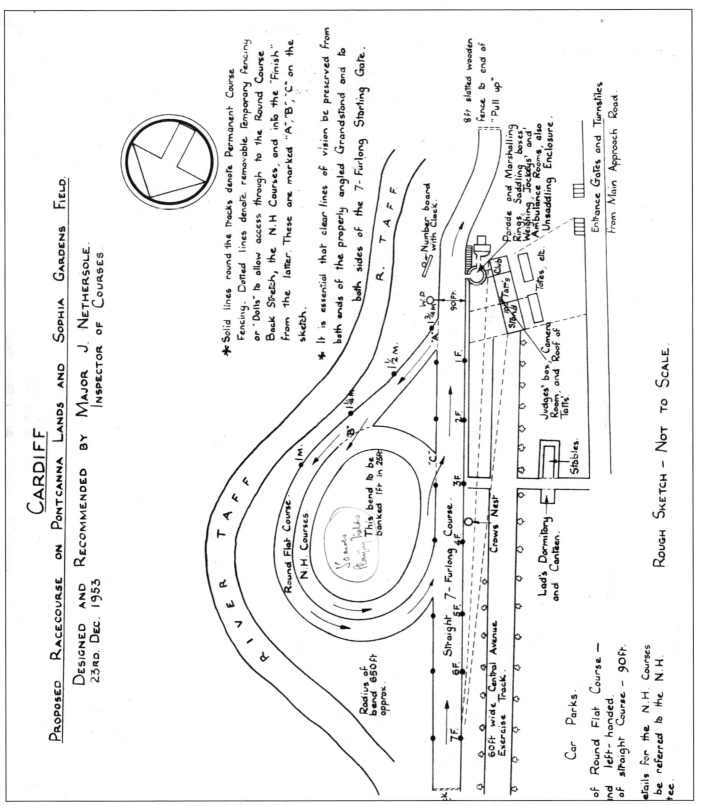

The racecourse that never was. A little known fact is that in the 1950s plans were drawn up for a new racecourse at Pontcanna and Sophia Gardens. Sadly, it never came about and, apart from one unlicensed meeting held in Sophia Gardens in 1958, Cardiff has had no horse racing since Ely Racecourse closed in 1939.

The magnificent Wales Empire Swimming Pool, built for the 1958 Empire and Commonwealth Games, was demolished to make way for the Millennium Stadium.

Susan Hanscombe is in no danger of drowning at the Wales Empire Swimming Pool with Olympic medallist Nick Gillingham (third from left) and three other males at hand, *c.*1985.

World of Work

Staff of Wadsworth Transport (Cardiff) Ltd. Third from the right back row is Mike Geary, 1944.

Workers at Lyons Ice Cream depot in Penarth Road. Third from left front row is Stanley MacCormac, 1955.

Cardiff GPO Engineering staff conference, *c.*1963.

Forty years ago in 1962 these members of Electrolux appear to have had a great time at their annual staff party.

Western Mail & Echo managing director David Cole (cigar in hand) says farewell to machine minder Ossie Evans (to his right). Others in the picture include Mac Beames, Danny Edwards, George Pearce, Charlie Lee, Albert Godwin, Chris Godwin, Ted Perryman, Robert Potter, Peter Clifton, Tony Gentile, George Renwick, Keith Jones, George Vanstone, Lenny Johnson, David Jones, John Haines, Stan Parsons, *c.*1961.

South Wales Echo dispatch worker Billy Lee receiving a retirement gift from Father of the Chapel (shop steward) Pat O'Brien in 1975. Some of his workmates looking on are Charlie Lee, Harry Collins, Frank Boyd, Billy James, Albert Johnson and Danny Rowlands.

The old method of etching plates for printing pictures when the *Western Mail & Echo* offices were situated in St Mary Street. In the centre is apprentice Harry Ferris who worked for the company for more than half-a-century and who retired in 1979 as manager of the process department. Tom Evans and Francome Williams (wearing spectacles) are the other workers, *c*.1931.

Western Mail & Echo process workers operating the German Hell Electronic machines at Thomson House in the 1970s.

Bill Smith park keeper at Alexandra Gardens, Cathays Park, gets a helping hand from this smartly dressed young lad, *c.*1949.

Stones from the banks of the old Glamorgan Canal were used in the construction of Maindy Stadium, *c.*1950.

Idris Evans's old horse
made it's last bread
delivery in the January
of 1958.

A chauffeur driven
Napier. There were no
parking problems when
this vehicle was seen on
the roads of Cardiff
before World War One.

Long skirts were all the fashion when these five young ladies who worked for Sir Percy Thomas & Son Architects, Cathedral Road, posed for this picture in 1955.

St Peter's Roman Catholic Church Parish Committee, *c.*1960.

In 1895 chief constables and inspectors stationed at Canton Police Station posed for this group photograph. Note the walruss moustaches!

Cardiff City Police new recruits, *c.*1920.

Cardiff City Police motor patrol, 1933.

Police cadets on parade, 1969.

Cardiff City Fire Brigade. In the centre is Superintendent G. Geen, *c.*1913.

Cardiff City Fire Brigade in action, *c.*1970.

Cardiff at War

This is how the houses numbered 33 to 43 St Agnes Road, Heath, looked after an air-raid in 1943.

These houses in Allensbank Road were also badly damaged.

Cardiff City Police ARP 1939 to 1945. Llandaff Court. You would have thought someone would have cut the grass!

Cardiff City Police CID, 1941-2.

These Oxford Street children enjoyed a victory tea party on 13 June 1946.

A fancy dress competition in Whitchurch was just one way of celebrating the end of World War Two.

John 'Jackie' Donovan and his brother Billy with their nephew Brian Lee in the garden of 23 Thesiger Street. Note the door to the air-raid shelter where Brian and his sister Valerie and their mother spent many sleepless nights during the war years.

The gentleman second from the right prepares to cut the cake at this VE-Day children's party in Ely.

Home Guard children's Christmas party at the Drill Hall, West Grove, 1942.

The smiles on the faces say it all! More end of World War Two celebrations, but this time at Pengam Green, Tremorfa.

Patrick Donovan, of 59
Frederick Street, served
with the Royal Welsh
Fusiliers in France
during World War
One. He had five sons
and three daughters.
Two of his sons, John
and Billy, are featured
on page 182. His
youngest son, Philip,
who served with the
RASC in Palestine
during World War
Two, is shown below.

During World War One, Whitchurch Mental Hospital was used as a military hospital. These convalescent soldiers can be seen enjoying some fresh air in the grounds of the hospital.

Celebrating peace at the Rhiwbina Village Recreation Club at the end of World War One.

Company Sergeant Major Fred Barter, of Daniel Street, who was awarded the Victoria Cross during World War One. On 16 May 1915, at Festubert having gained the first line of enemy trenches, he called for volunteers, and with eight gallant men attacked the German position with bombs, capturing three officers, 102 men, and around 500 yards of enemy trenches. He later found and cut 11 of the German mine leads.

Welsh troops leaving Cardiff Castle during World War One.

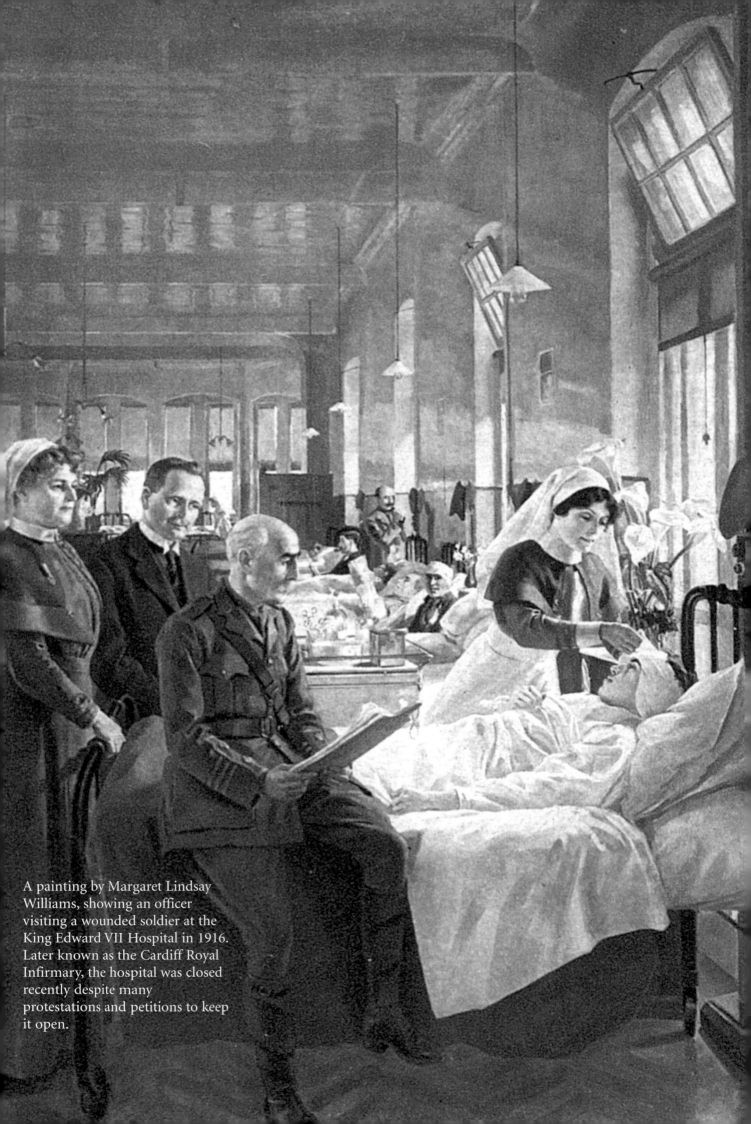

A painting by Margaret Lindsay Williams, showing an officer visiting a wounded soldier at the King Edward VII Hospital in 1916. Later known as the Cardiff Royal Infirmary, the hospital was closed recently despite many protestations and petitions to keep it open.

Soldiers marching past the Cardiff Soldiers Rest in St Mary Street during World War One.

Presentation to the City of Cardiff of a German gun captured at Loos by the Welsh Guards, 18 November 1915.

Happiest Days of Their Lives?

After the end of World War One, these schoolchildren from Rhiwbina posed for this delightful picture.

Children playing Ring a Ring of Roses in Rhiwbina before World War Two.

The girls of Rhiwbina Infants School appear to have outnumbered the boys in 1974.

Rhiwbina Kindergarten children before setting out for a walk in the 1970s.

Old Ely schoolchildren pictured in 1933.

Schoolgirls from St David's Roman Catholic School waiting for the paddle steamer to Weston-super-Mare. Fourth from the right is Mary Johnson. The names of some of the other girls are Chrissie Davies, Vera Clements, Pat Kelly, Rita Milton, Mary Hopkins, Sheila Bulpin and Mary Collins, *c.*1939.

These two photographs show some rather well dressed children from Wood Street School in the 1920s.

St David's Roman Catholic School infants class. Second right front row is John 'Jackie' Donovan, *c*.1931.

These young pupils of Gladstone School attended a concert during World War Two.

Forms three and four Gladstone Boys School, December 1946.

Gladstone Boys School, 1947. Left to right: R. Duggan, T. Walker, A. Williams, G. Garrett.

Rhiwbina Kindergarten children's nativity play, *c.*1975.

Eglwys Newydd School pupils, 1982.

Eglwys Newydd School music class, 1982.

Whitchurch High School, 1983.

Whitchurch High School, form 4B, 1982.

Eglwys Newydd School boys choir, 1983.

Children of Whitchurch Judo Club, *c.*1984.

Leisure and Pleasure

The cast of *Who Goes There?* St Peter's Theatre Group, October 1955.

St Peter's Youth Club Hallowen party, 31 October 1958.

Curran's tennis team which was coached by Stanley MacCormac (third left), April 1955.

Motorbike trials at Rhiwbina in the 1920s.

Enjoying a Christmas time drink in the Carlton Hotel are, left to right, Jackie Godfrey, unknown, Teddy Connolly, Mary and Philip Donovan, *c.*1950.

Cardiff City Police annual dinner and ball, 1954.

The Lord Mayor with Clara Novello Davies and her Royal Welsh Ladies Choir prior to their departure for the Paris Exposition on 16 October 1937.

Waldini's Gipsy Band was popular with Cardiffians in the 1930s.

The popular Admiral Napier in Canton was partly underwater when this photograph was taken in the 1960s.

Sally Williams, aged 15, seen standing in the snow outside the Monico Cinema which is destined for closure, 1982.

Hollywood film star Gene Autry *The Singing Cowboy* shakes hands with the Lord Mayor Richard Gruffyd Robinson on his visit to the city in 1947.

The Coronet Cinema in Woodville Road opened in 1914 and closed in 1958. Thousands of children enjoyed the Gene Autry films that were shown there at Saturday matinees. The cinema was demolished in 1972 to make way for a petrol station and a block of flats now stands on the spot.

The Plaza on North Road opened 1928 and closed in 1981. A retirement housing complex now stands on the site.

This was the Globe Cinema in Wellfield Road three years before it closed in 1985. It opened in March 1910 and was demolished soon after its closure despite a petition to save the Grade II listed building.

Cardiffians have been flocking to the New Theatre ever since it opened in 1906 for all kinds of entertainment from pantomime to opera.

After his successful West End debut in *The Hobbit*, Michael Geary (MacCormac) from Whitchurch, was back in the role of Bilbo Baggins at the New Theatre. He is seen here with co-star Andy Williams as Gandalf, The Wizard.